are you wife ready?
small group curriculum

leader guide

*Preparing women for marriage
beyond the wedding day*

kim mcQuitty

Wife Ready
110 Walter Way, Suite #1751
Stockbridge, GA 30281
www.wiferead.org
info@wiferead.org

Library of Congress Cataloging-in Publication Data

Cover and author's photograph by Marielle McQuitty www.mariellemcquitty.com

Design and layout by Davyn Riley

Printed in the United States of America

for marielle and simone

testimonials about wife ready...

"I came out of this experience a whole person and with the BIBLICAL perspective of marriage and what it is to be a wife!" – Michelle M.

"This small group is a complete and utter blessing! It taught me not only what it means to be a wife but how to value myself as a woman! The workbook is full and is a wealth of knowledge that I couldn't and wouldn't obtain anywhere else! This NEEDS to be a global ministry! Marriages would greatly benefit from it!" – Jennifer A.

"You've truly helped me transform my life from a miserable single to a healthy whole single!" – Kim P.

"The Wife Ready Small Group caused me to closely examine myself and consider the barriers that exist in my life that prevent me from developing the relationship that I desire." – Ashley P.

"The Word of God was presented in a loving manner but at the same time it challenged me to do the work in order to grow and become ready to be a wife." – Wendy L.

"This superseded what I had expected. I've completed many single's seminars in the past but this one went deeper. It brought out suppressed feelings of issues that I dealt with as a child, preteen and teenager. I thought I had gotten over them but during the sessions and completing the homework assignments, I had to deal with the hard reality that I'm not over them and that I need the Holy Spirit to help me to get through it so that I can be healed and prepared for the husband God has for me." – Brittany B.

"My most valuable takeaway was 'the happier I am as a single right now; will be how happy I'll be in a relationship and future marriage.' So, it's necessary that I become whole, complete and work on me as much as I can as a single." – Rebecca W.

"My life has been impacted in a greater way. I'm not only preparing for a wedding, but just being that Proverbs 31 woman altogether. I've healed so much! The little girl in me was finally freed on day one of the session and I'm glad I was able to be at peace with where I am." – Karen J.

contents

a personal note from Kim i

leader's guide
how to lead...iii
preparing to lead...vii
session overview...xxi

group roster..xxxi

prayer requests.....................................xxxiii

session 1 - who are you?..........................3
identity
purpose

session 2 - are you whole?......................27
wholeness
healing

session 3 - the right one........................45
mr. right
the wait

session 4 - sexual purity 71
worth and value
sex is God's idea
soul ties

session 5 - wife material 89
are you a wife?
biblical roles

session 6 - marriage 109
what marriage is
what marriage is not

session 7 - final thoughts 129
dear wife-to-be

appendix 143
affirmations
how to avoid falling into sexual temptation
purity contract
questions to ask before you say, "I do"
31 prayers for my future husband

about the author 179

endnotes 180

kim mcQuitty

a personal note from Kim...

Thank you for partnering with me as a small group leader to help prepare God's daughters for marriage. Marriage will be the most important human relationship the women in your group will have in their lifetime; you will play a part.

The vision of *Wife Ready* is to provide women with the opportunity to learn and receive guidance about marriage *before* they say "I do." The premise of *Wife Ready* is if the potential wife is happy, healthy, healed, whole and complete, the better their marriage will be.

God is looking for women to pour into His daughters. In Titus 2:5, He admonishes the older women to teach the younger women. Whether you are older in age or older in experience, you can impact lives because a woman doesn't automatically know how to be a wife or mother.

Women today have little knowledge concerning what the Bible says about building a marriage, managing a home and caring for a family. Many have never seen a great example of a godly marriage modeled before them. Some came from broken or dysfunctional homes and may be afraid they will repeat the same pattern. Many are fatherless daughters looking for a man to give them what their father couldn't, and have no clue how problems from their past will affect their marriage. There is so much brokenness; so much healing is needed.

This is why they need you. What are some things you learned from the difficult times in your marriage? What has the Bible taught you about being a wife? What can you share that will change the trajectory of a young woman's life in your group? You have a story. You have a testimony. Be prepared to share it so others can walk in freedom.

Give them insights from your own marriage relationship and the freedom to ask questions. You don't have to share private and intimate events from your marriage. However, you should lead the group with transparency as this is how transformation and healing take place. Women need to hear the truth about marriage; no more fallacies and myths. They need the wisdom and guidance of someone who is, or has been married, to point them in the right direction. They need someone with compassion to coach them - not preach to them - and help prepare them for the journey. They need you!

kim mcQuitty

how to lead

You don't need years of training, a life coach certification or a special degree to be a *Wife Ready* facilitator. All you need is the willingness to be available to impart wisdom, empower and equip women to enter marriage with their eyes wide open, and make an informed, biblical decision on who they will spend the rest of their lives with.

Leading isn't about telling a young woman your thoughts about marriage, but rather God's heartbeat for it. It is instructing her from the Word of God. The blueprint for being a wife can be found in prayer. The manual is the Word of God.

The 80/20 rule of facilitating is for you to listen more and talk less. This will allow an organic flow of the group discussion.

Carefully read through the workbook and leader's guide. Familiarize yourself with each session. Emphasize to your group the importance of completing the Ready Work assignments which is their weekly homework. This is where they discover the truth about themselves and how transformation and healing will take place. Make certain to let the participants know they will only get out of this study what they put in.

If an issue arises for which you are ill-equipped to handle, simply pass the information along to your churches' small group leader. We want every woman to experience the healing she needs.

Finally, use the roster I have provided to collect the names, email addresses and prayer requests from the ladies in your group for you to stay in touch with them. Pray for them. Give them your contact information; share your prayer request as well. Show them you care and are available to them not just during this study but long after it is over.

requirements

as a *Wife Ready* facilitator:

- **You must be currently or previously married a minimum of 3 years. You cannot lead where you haven't been.**

- Open and close each meeting in prayer

- Allow the Holy Spirit to lead and guide you

- Have a basic biblical understanding of marriage

- Be willing to acknowledge problems and successes in marriage

- Having previous participation in small group leadership, and a good knowledge of how they operate is helpful, but not required

- Be prepared to facilitate each session and keep the discussion conversational

- Lead from your own experience

- Create a safe environment for women to share.

- What is said in the group stays in the group

- Thank them for sharing during the discussion time

- Remember the 80/20 rule

as a *Wife Ready* facilitator <u>do</u> <u>not</u>:

- Use this group as a time to bash your husband or speak negatively about men or marriage

- Dominate conversations with your experience about your current or previous relationships or marriage

- Counsel women. Leave that to the leaders of your church.

- Allow participants to cross talk or dominate the conversations.

- Act as if you have all the answers. Be honest when you don't.

- Give your personal opinion of someone's current dating situation

- Discourage women from marriage out of your own hardships

preparing to lead

1. First, pray! Before you can lead, your heart needs to be prepared. That begins with prayer.

2. Prepare beforehand to lead the sessions. Spend some time each week previewing the video and going over these leader notes so you will be ready for a great group experience.

3. Encourage attendance. A valuable asset of being in a small group is to build community with other women who are in the same or similar season of life. Encourage them not to miss a session, if possible.

4. Before you begin the first session, share a little about yourself so the participants can get to know you. Explain how this study works and how they will get the most from it.

5. You may want to provide refreshments; however, this is completely up to you. If you choose to, moving forward you can delegate the responsibility to the ladies.

6. Your weekly *Wife Ready* small group will be built around the following components: (1) video lesson and (2) group discussion questions.

    Each video session is taught by Kim, and will be 5-10 minutes in length. The videos are available as a digital download which can be viewed within your group on a computer, iPad, or an Internet enabled television with a streaming device such as Apple TV, Fire TV, Chromecast or Roku.

7. On the following pages are the discussion questions so you can lead each session with confidence. This course is designed so that the video teaching and the discussion questions will fit into a one-hour segment.

8. Homework! During the week, emphasize the importance of completing the homework entitled, Ready Work. This is where healing, enlightenment and transformation will occur individually as they prepare themselves for marriage.

    Allow those who desire to share from their homework the opportunity to do so. The Bible says in Revelation 12:11, *"And they overcame him by the blood of the Lamb and by the word of their testimony..."* As they share what God is doing in them, others in the group will be ministered to.

9. When asking the ladies what their biggest takeaway is from the video session, allow the discussion to continue as naturally as possible. You may need to start the ball rolling by sharing what part was most applicable to your marriage or life journey.

10. I have included additional *Wife Ready* resources in the Appendix that will serve the ladies long after the group time has ended. Encourage the participates to use them.

11. Lastly, encourage the women to take advantage of reading my book entitled, *Unsave The Date, Are You Wife Ready*. It isn't required to complete this small group curriculum; however, it will be tremendously beneficial to them as they prepare for marriage. The book can be ordered from wifeready.org.

session overview

kim mcQuitty

week 1
session 1 - who are you?

Open in prayer. Introduce yourself. Get acquainted with the participants by using the icebreakers below. Provide an overview of the curriculum and how this study works. Watch Session 1, then use the discussion questions to guide the conversation.

icebreakers

- What is your current status: single, single again, dating, or engaged.

- Good or bad, what are some things you have learned from a previous relationship?

- What do you hope to gain from this curriculum?

are you wife ready? small group curriculum leader guide

Main objective: Knowing your purpose and who you are is important to discover before committing the rest of one's life to someone else. Their worth and value is in who they are in Christ. He completes them, not a man.

group discussion questions:

- What is one thing that really stood out to you on the video?

- What does it mean to understand your worth and value?

- Why is it important to know who you are?

- How active are you in living your life versus passively waiting for a husband?

week 2
session 2 - are you whole?

Open in prayer. Ask the ladies for feedback from their Ready Work. Watch Session 2, then use the discussion questions to guide the conversation.

Main objective: You cannot have a healthy relationship with someone else until you have one first with yourself. You must be healed and whole before entering marriage; not a fragment of who God created you to be.

group discussion questions:

- What would you like to share that was most meaningful to you from your Ready Work?

- What is one thing that really stood out to you on the video?

- How have you made the connection with who you are and what may have occurred in your life?

- Can you identify any brokenness in your life that will impact your marriage? Share it with the group.

week 3
session 3 - the right one

Open in prayer. Ask the ladies for feedback from their Ready Work. Watch Session 3, then use the discussion questions to guide the conversation.

Main objective: The success of one's marriage is predicated upon marrying the right person. God has a man who is suitable for them, but they must invite Him into their selection process.

group discussion questions:

- What would you like to share that was most meaningful to you from your Ready Work?

- What is one thing that really stood out to you on the video?

- What are your thoughts on God's ability to choose a mate for you now, who is exactly what you'll still need decades later?

- What could be the fate of your marriage if you choose your partner independent of God?

week 4
session 4 - sexual purity

Open in prayer. Ask the ladies for feedback from their Ready Work. Watch Session 4, then use the discussion questions to guide the conversation.

Main objective: God knows more about sex than we do. The parameters He placed around sex are to protect you not deprive you.

group discussion questions:

- What would you like to share that was most meaningful to you from your Ready Work?

- What is one thing that really stood out to you on the video?

- Understanding what a soul tie is, how does that put some things into perspective for you?

- What are your thoughts on the questions Kim asked about engaging in premarital sex?

premarital sex questions

The next time you are faced with the decision to have sex outside of marriage ask yourself?

- Do I want to deal with a soul tie?

- Do I want to honor God with my body?

- Do I believe I know more about sex than God does?

- Do I want to open the door to the enemy in my life through my sin?

- Do I want to open my spirit to every woman, this man has ever slept with?

- Do I want to instill the seed of insecurity into my life?

- Do I want to be riddled with shame and guilt?

- Do I want to be separated from God?

- Do I want to grieve the Holy Spirit?

week 5
session 5 - wife material

Open in prayer. Ask the ladies for feedback from their Ready Work. Watch Session 5, then use the discussion questions to guide the conversation.

Main objective: You can become a wife BEFORE you are married. Marriage is a condition of the heart, not just a marital status.

group discussion questions:

- What would you like to share that was most meaningful to you from your Ready Work?

- What is one thing that really stood out to you on the video?

- What are your thoughts on the biblical roles that God will require of you as a wife?

- How you will make the mental shift from "me to we"?

week 6
session 6 – marriage

Open in prayer. Ask the ladies for feedback from their Ready Work. Watch Session 6, then use the discussion questions to guide the conversation.

Main objective: God created marriage to reflect the relationship that Christ has with the church. Marriage is a covenant and not a contract.

group discussion questions:

- What would you like to share that was most meaningful to you from your Ready Work?

- What is one thing that really stood out to you on the video?

- What are your thoughts on Kim's analogy of marriage being like a final sale?

- Explain the difference between a contract and a covenant.

week 7
session 7 – final thoughts

Open in prayer. Ask the ladies for feedback from their Ready Work. Watch Session 7, then use the discussion questions to guide the conversation.

Main objective: Kim give's her final thoughts on being *wife ready*.

group discussion questions

- What would you like to share that was most meaningful to you from your Ready Work?

- What are your overall thoughts about this Wife Ready experience?

kim mcQuitty

group roster

Name	Email	Phone
....	....	....
....	....	....
....	....	....
....	....	....
....	....	....
....	....	....
....	....	....
....	....	....
....	....	....
....	....	....
....	....	....
....	....	....

prayer requests

Name ....

Request ....

....

....

....

Name ....

Request ....

....

....

....

Name ....

Request ....

....

....

....

Name ....

Request ....
....
....
....

Name ....

Request ....
....
....
....

Name ....

Request ....
....
....
....

kim mcQuitty

Name ....

Request ....

....

....

....

Name ....

Request ....

....

....

....

Name ....

Request ....

....

....

....

Name ....

Request ....

....

....

....

Name ....

Request ....

....

....

....

Name ....

Request ....

....

....

....

session 1
who are you?

1

who are you?

"…and you are complete in Him, who is the head of all principality and power."
Colossians 2:10 (NKJV)

"Your identity must be rooted in Christ and the finished work on the cross. You cannot look for it anywhere else or in anyone else. God created you with a portion of your soul that only He can fill. Nothing or no one will ever be able to fill it. No career, no ministry, no child, and no amount of money can fill that place in your life or complete you. If you attempt to fill that longing with anything other than God, you will be in a repetitive cycle of dissatisfaction and emptiness." – *Unsave The Date*, Chapter 2, page 24.

identity

From a young girl, we aspire to be married. We daydreamed and perhaps have even journaled about it. Many have created a self-imposed timeline of when they expect to be married, and formed their identity around the expectation of being a wife.

When marriage doesn't happen by a certain age, we tend to think something is wrong with us, and feel incomplete because of our deep longing to be married.

We rehearse questions and statements like, "Why am I still single?" "Why haven't I been chosen by now?" "I thought for certain I would have been a wife and mother by this age!" "I'm not getting any younger and my biological clock is ticking."

Marriage is a beautiful relationship. However, it does not define who you are as a woman. Just because you are single, doesn't mean you are incomplete. Let that sink in! If you are in Christ, you are complete, entire, full and lacking nothing! Colossians 2:10 (NKJV) says, *"...for in Him you are complete."*

It is important to define yourself by your relationship in Christ, and not by your circumstances. When your relationship with Christ is strong, you become secure in your worth and value. On the other hand, when you lack the confidence of knowing who you are in Christ, you look for it from outside sources to define you. Knowing who you are is an inside job. You don't need validation from anyone. If God is not enough, no man will ever be.

You are a daughter of the King! You already have everything you need in the person of Jesus, right now--today! You don't need a man to complete you because you are already complete in Christ.

4

God created marriage for us to enjoy. There are tremendous blessings in having a husband and family. Marriage also is a gift wrapped in responsibility. It's not a necessity.

I understand the longing in your heart to be married, God placed it there because we were created for relationships. But please understand the importance of knowing who you are, so that you don't use marriage as an attempt to complete yourself. Marriage is a relationship you get to enjoy; you don't need it to be complete!

You need to know what your unique personality traits, strengths and weaknesses are. If you don't have a clue what they are, how do you know what kind of person you need or would like for a partner? The more you know yourself, the clearer your sense of inner direction will be when it comes to finding the love of your life. What do you enjoy? What are your values? What's important to you? Spend your time while you're single getting to know yourself and loving the wonderful woman God created in His image – the woman He intends for you to be.

purpose

You have a destiny to fulfill and it's more than being a wife and a mother. There is something God has called every one of us to do.

So, who are you? What is the "why" of your life? What is your purpose? Why are you here?

Jeremiah 29:11-13 (NIV) says, *"For I know the plans I have for you, declares the Lord, plans for welfare and not for calamity to give you a future and a hope. Then you will call upon Me and come and pray to me and I will listen to you. You will see me and find Me when you search for Me with all your heart."*

God has a plan and purpose for your life. When you are doing what He has called you to do, you will find fulfillment in that. I'm not saying you won't ever feel lonely, you will. Again, we were all created for relationships. However, when you're walking in purpose you aren't so consumed with getting married that you neglect the very reason for your existence.

On judgment day, you will stand before God as an individual to give an account for your life, not as husband and wife. God will ask what did you do with the gifts, purpose and assignment He placed in you. This is why, as a single woman, you should be actively living your life, not passively waiting for a husband. You have a destiny to fulfill. Your focus shouldn't be on the need to be in a relationship with a man, but rather on cultivating your relationship with the Son of Man, Jesus Christ, while doing what He told you to do.

If you marry a man who is "suitable" for you (we talk more about that in a later session) he should want you to be the highest expression of what God has created you to be, and help you obtain that. Knowing the purpose that God is requiring you to fulfill is vital. If you marry a man who will compliment your purpose and not compete with it, because you belong to God first, he will understand your life is not solely about being his wife.

"The greatest tragedy in life is not death, but a life without a purpose."

Dr. Myles Munroe

"The only thing a man should want to change about you is your last name. You should be the highest expression of yourself in a marriage, not a fraction of who God made you to be."

Kim McQuitty
@wifeready

session 1
ready work

You should have a set of clearly written and prioritized core values that guide your daily life and define who you are. What are your core values?   List seven of them.

What is your purpose in life? What were you put on earth to do?

What does it mean to you to be "complete in Christ?"

What part of your personality do you believe will be problematic in your relationship?

How will you manage this?

kim mcQuitty

know thyself

The journey to know yourself is one everyone should take.

The preparation for marriage must first be met with becoming well aware of all the special features that make you the unique individual you are. This journaling exercise will help you know and understand who you really are. There are no right or wrong answers.

Who is the most important person in your life, and why?

How do you feel about yourself—physically, emotionally, mentally, and spiritually?

What are you passionate about?

What do you like to do for fun?

When do you feel afraid most?

Are you happy with your life? If not, why?

What is your relationship like with Jesus and what is His role in your life?

What are your three strongest qualities?

How do you want your life to be remembered?

What causes you anxiety?

Describe yourself in one word.

Describe the person you see when you look in the mirror.

What do you want your legacy to be?

What is an accomplishment that makes you proud of yourself?

kim mcQuitty

What makes you happy?

Who is your greatest influence?

What are five words that define you?

What motivates you?

How would you describe your ability to manage stress?

What would you like to learn if you had the chance?

When do you feel lonely? How do you manage it?

What is your weakest quality?

kim mcQuitty

How do you define love?

What makes you sad?

How hard is it to say "no?"

What can't you live without?

are you wife ready? small group curriculum

What makes you feel insecure?

How do you define "home?"

"Christ
completes you,
not a man."

Kim McQuitty

@wifeready

"A woman who knows her worth and value will not allow her life to hang in the balance indefinitely with a man who will not commit his life to hers."

Kim McQuitty

@wifeready

kim mcQuitty

notes

notes

kim mcQuitty

notes

notes

session 2
are you whole?

2

are you whole?

"He heals the wounds of every shattered heart." Psalm 147:3 (TPT)

"You must deal with the brokenness and unresolved issues in your life. If not, you will oftentimes find yourself repeating a cycle of frustration and dysfunction that, in turn, limits and can even destroy intimacy. Intimacy is unhindered access and emotional closeness. True love cannot flow through your heart when it is clogged with fear, pain and hurt." *Unsave the Date*, Chapter 3, page 4.

wholeness

One of the ingredients necessary for a happy marriage is to deal with the issues of your past. Les Parrott, Ph.D. states in his book, *Saving Your Marriage Before It Starts*, "Marriage won't make you happy, you make marriage happy."

We all have experienced some type of brokenness, trauma, or deep hurt in our lives that really stung and left pocket of pain. Yours may have occurred when you were a young girl and still pollutes your relationships today. Did your mom or dad reject or abandon you? Did they divorce? Did you lose a parent at a young age? Did someone violate you? Were you verbally abused? Or, perhaps later in life, a former boyfriend or ex-husband cheated on you? I'm sorry that happened to you. You didn't deserve that.

Maybe your brokenness wasn't as traumatic, but what you experienced scarred you and left a residue of mistrust in your heart. Perhaps you weren't raised or loved well, or maybe the environment or culture in which you grew up left you predisposed to a toxic way of thinking.

Regardless of the brokenness or pocket of pain you experienced, if it hasn't been healed, it will leave you in a cycle that keeps you stuck from moving forward. Brokenness explains why you have the life issues you have. It is the reason for a lot of your relationship problems, and why you may be caught in unhealthy cycles going through the same thing over and over.

Life events have a way of shaping us into something we were never meant to be. It effects how you think and feel about yourself and the lens through which you see life. It impacts the way you act and respond. That trauma or event you encountered forever changed the trajectory of your life. Left unhealed, that pain will result in a lifetime of bleeding which often causes you to unintentionally hurt others.

Choosing not to deal with a painful or eventful past won't make it go away. You must deal with it because you cannot conquer what you will not confront! You have to feel it to heal it. If it hasn't been dealt with properly, your past is your present because it affects today in a negative manner.

It is vital to the health of your marriage that you are healed and whole before you say, "I do." If you aren't a whole and healed individual before you get married, marriage won't make you one. Brokenness brought into a marriage is one of the reasons why many marriages fail. You cannot have a healthy relationship with someone else until you are healed. True love and intimacy cannot flow from a heart that is filled with fear and pain.

healing

The pain that you experienced was not your fault; however, your healing is your responsibility. Wholeness is not an option; it's mandatory if you want to have a thriving marriage relationship. You have to enter marriage as a whole individual; not a fragment of who God created you to be.

"So, how do I get free?" I'm glad you asked. The first step in the healing process is forgiveness. Begin today by choosing to forgive those who may have hurt you. Release them. Whether they have asked for your forgiveness or not. Set yourself free by forgiving them anyway. Allow the Lord to heal your heart. Only the healing power of Jesus Christ can heal and make you whole again. You must allow Him into those broken areas if you want to be healed. Psalm 147:3 (TPT) says, *"He heals the wounds of every shattered heart."* Regardless of the extent you've been wounded, He can make you whole again.

Next, you will have to renew your mind. Romans 12:2 (NKJV) says, *"And do not be conformed to this world, but be transformed by the renewing of your mind, so that you may prove what the will of God is, that which is good and acceptable and perfect."*

The transformation you need will occur when the strongholds keeping you in bondage are broken. A stronghold is a wrong pattern of thinking that produces a wrong pattern of living. What lies have you believed as a result of what happened to you? Counteract those lies with the truth of God's Word. This is how you renew your mind.

It was not your fault! You are not damaged goods. You are worthy of being deeply loved and cherished. You *can* trust people with your heart again because everyone isn't out to hurt you. You no longer have to live in fear and self-protection.

When completing your homework this week, take some time to reflect on any pain that has occurred in your life. Pray and ask God to reveal the areas where your brokenness has impeded your progress or stifled you in any way. Allow His love to envelope you. He has an awesome plan for your life. Next, get in your Bible. Locate the Scriptures which speak the truth that will bring healing. Meditate on them until transformation occurs. This transformation will begin with how you think.

Finally, use the affirmations in the Appendix to help you shatter any lies. The power is in consistency, so say them daily. What you repeatedly hear you will eventually believe.

"Get yourself healthy before you get yourself married."

Dr. Neil Clark Warren

session 2
ready work

Who are the people in your life you've needed to forgive?

Have you forgiven them? If yes, how?

Who do you still need to forgive?

Have you truly forgiven yourself of any past mistakes? If yes, how did you do that? If no, why not?

If you were hurt in a previous relationship, describe how have you healed?

In what ways have you forgiven your ex-spouse, ex-boyfriend, or ex-fiancé?

What are some of the signs you have ignored in past relationships?

Why did you ignore the signs?

What were the consequences?

What were lessons you learned?

Why would you choose a relationship with someone with whom you know is not good for you?

What would you do differently in your next relationship you did not do in a previous one?

If you are divorced, how have you taken responsibility for the demise of your marriage?

How have you dealt with childhood wounds you have acquired, i.e. rejection, abandonment, daddy and/or momma issues, emotional deprivation, and any physical and/or sexual abuse?

"Getting married won't heal the pain from your past, confronting the truth and dealing with the hurt does."

Kim McQuitty

@wifeready

kim mcQuitty

notes

notes

kim mcQuitty

notes

are you wife ready? small group curriculum

notes

session 3
the right one

3

the right one

"Then the LORD God said, It is not good for the man to be alone; I will make a helper suitable for him." Genesis 2:18 (NASB)

"Single ladies, take your time in moving forward with a man who you believe could be "the one" God has chosen for you. While there is no "perfect will" versus "permissible will" when it comes down to God's will and mate for your life, there is someone who is more suitable for you." – *Unsave the Date*, Chapter 2, page 33.

mr. right

The success of your marriage is dependent upon you marrying the right man for you. Everything God does is intentional and with purpose, including marriage. Marriage is more than you having a man. There is a purpose for your marriage which is why it is vital that you marry the one who is 'His best' for your life.

According to Genesis 2:18, there is a man who is more suitable for you according to the plan He has for your union.

I'm not implying there is only one man out of the 3.5 billion men on the earth for you. However, there is one man who is more suitable, complementary, tailor-made and just right for you according to God's purpose for your life and marriage.

I'm often asked, "How do I know if he's the one?" My answer, "You just know." Any married couple will tell you the same thing. Is it that simple? Yes, it is! Just like you know the last one wasn't, you'll know who the right one is, as long as you allow God into your selection process.

In your finite mind, you are not smart enough to choose a man 'today,' who will still be suitable for you 'decades' into the future. You don't have enough wisdom and insight to make a lifelong decision that gets better year after year. Only a loving Father, in His infinite wisdom and omniscience is able to do that. He takes into consideration what you desire in a mate, blends it with what He knows is best, and sends that man to find you.

God knows what His purpose is for your life. He knew what He planned for you before your momma and daddy planned or unplanned to have you! So, why would you make a selection without His consideration and direction? Proverbs 19:21 (NIV) says, *"Many are the plans in a man's heart, but it's the Lord's purpose that prevails."*

the wait

Waiting for the right guy to find you can be hard, no doubt. We were created for relationships and it's a natural longing to be in one. However, when you've been waiting for years, the wait becomes a weight. At times your heart may get heavy having to always show up to functions and holidays alone. Some of you have been waiting much longer than you thought you'd ever have to, and others are back in the waiting room after the demise of a marriage. It can be a lonely and trying time.

There is an advantage, however, to being single. Use this time for growth, personal development and to focus on your relationship with the Lord. 1 Corinthians 7:34 (NIV) says, *"….In the same way, a woman who is no longer married or has never been married can be devoted to the Lord and holy in body and in spirit. But a married woman has to think about her earthly responsibilities and how to please her husband."* Use this time of being single to live life to the fullest and work on yourself. Once you're married, your priorities will shift. The best gift you can offer your future husband is a healthy, whole, healed and a happy you.

As you date, take your time getting to know him. Dating should be a time of intent and establishing trust. Have fun of course, but be intentional. If somewhere along the line, there is an unsettling in your spirit, don't push past that. If you have more uncertainty than peace, don't gloss over that. Refuse to continue in a relationship that isn't going anywhere out of fear that another guy won't come along. Don't let fear rob you of God's best and marry someone you know isn't right for you. It's better to wait long than to marry wrong.

Your prayer should be, "Lord if he's not from You, I don't want him." Choose to remain single until who you prayed for finds you. If you wait right, you'll only have to wait once. And knowing God like I do, I promise, the right one will be worth the wait.

On the following pages are questions to ask yourself about a potential Mr. Right.

"The success of your marriage hinges on marrying the right person for you. Just because you are attracted, doesn't mean you are compatible."

Kim McQuitty
@wiferedy

"Don't try to
find the one.
Spend your
time becoming
the one worth
finding."

Johnson Bowie
@johnsonbowie

session 3
ready work

What are your ten "must have" qualities in a man you would consider spending the rest of your life with?

1.

2.

3.

4.

5.

6.

7.

8.

9.

10.

What are your ten "must not have" qualities in a mate?

1.

2.

3.

4.

5.

6.

7.

8.

9.

10.

If you are in a relationship, how many of your "must haves" does your potential mate possess?

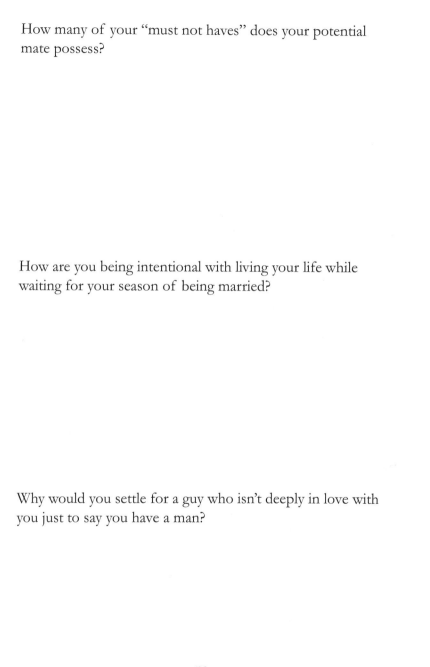

kim mcQuitty

How many of your "must not haves" does your potential mate possess?

How are you being intentional with living your life while waiting for your season of being married?

Why would you settle for a guy who isn't deeply in love with you just to say you have a man?

How long are you willing to date before you receive a proposal?

What are you basing this timeline on?

What will you say to the guy you have been dating for an extended period of time when it seems like he's dragging his feet about marriage?

the right one questionnaire

Below are questions to ask yourself about your potential mate. You will need to have spent a significant amount of time dating before you can honestly answer these questions. If you aren't in a serious relationship, this will be for a later time.

Pay attention to your answers and don't make excuses for him. If most of them don't lean toward what you desire in a mate, you may need to continue to wait. Time is always on your side when making the important decision of entering into marriage.

what do you have in common?

Do you share common life goals and visions?

What are those goals?

Do you have the same values?

What are those values?

Do you share the same faith?

are you on the same page?

How is your relationship built on mutual dreams and interests?

How does your family feel about him?

How satisfied are you with his drive to accomplish things in life compared to yours?

emotional wholeness

How is your emotional well-being and happiness independent of him?

How is his emotional well-being and happiness independent of you?

Everyone brings some baggage into the relationships. What baggage are you bringing? What baggage is he bringing? And how big is the bag...a backpack, a carryon or a suitcase or a trunk? Explain.

why him?

Other than physical attraction, why are you attracted to him?

Can you be honest about whether you are looking for to him to fill a need or void in your life? If so, what is it?

Why do you want to spend the rest of your life with him?

How do you feel when you are with him?

kim mcQuitty

How does he make you a better person?

What don't you like about him?

Are you willing to live with these issues for the rest of your life?

How have you determined these issues won't become problematic long-term?

How do you know you're in love with him?

"The one thing you will change about your man is his marital status."

Kim McQuitty
@wifeready

"If you wait right, you'll only have to wait once."

Kim McQuitty
@wifeready

kim mcQuitty

notes

notes

kim mcQuitty

notes

notes

session 4
sexual purity

4

sexual purity

"How can a man keep his way pure? By keeping it according to your word."
Psalm 119:9 (NASB)

"God created sex. It was His idea and a great one at that! He created it to be enjoyed within the relationship of a husband and wife. In today's culture, waiting until marriage to enjoy sex is antiquated. It's rare, uncommon and unheard of. We live in a hypersexual culture and the majority of sexually active people aren't married. The Bible is clear on God's stance on this topic, and He has not changed His mind regardless of what society says and does." -- *Unsave the Date*, Chapter 5, page 86.

worth and value

In order to walk in sexual purity, you need to understand your worth and value, with the help of the Holy Spirit. If you have repeatedly struggled in the area of sexual purity, chances are you have experienced some brokenness in your life. Ask Him to show you where you may be broken. Until He restores your soul and the trauma from your past, you will remain in sexual sin and perpetuate the cycle of unhealthy relationships. Only God can truly set you free and make you whole.

You are far more than giving yourself away to a man who has not made a covenant with you. Proverbs 31:10 (KJV) - *"Who can find a virtuous woman? For her price is far above rubies."* When you understand your worth and value, and establish the Word of God as your standard and source of authority, you won't allow just any man to take you into the bedroom. You won't compromise yourself for the sake of keeping him. Don't give yourself away with the hope of a commitment and loyalty; it won't work. You are better than that!

If a man's life isn't governed by the Word of God, he can't lead you. If he tries to lure you away from the Word, he's not the one. A man of God will have godly intentions and is also pursuing a life of abstinence. He will love God and honor you. Being involved with someone should never pull you away from God or cause you to compromise what you believe just to be with them.

So, what will be your standard of authority? On what will you base the philosophy of your life? Are you going to make a commitment to God's Word as your standard or are you going to make up your own? Are you committed more to what God says about you, or to what you think will meet your own needs?

Regardless of your sexual past, God has an awesome future for you. Choose to make a commitment according to God's standard. The rewards are profound!

sex is God's idea

God created sex to be enjoyed within the marriage covenant between a male and female. To say that He knows more about sex than we do, is an understatement. I could go on and on with what you already know, and that being, sex outside of marriage is a sin and sin separates you from God. However, I want to share a Kingdom perspective on this controversial subject, and give you something to think about as it pertains to premarital sex.

Everything God does He does from a place of love. He didn't put parameters around sex to deprive you but rather to protect you. He will not force these boundaries on you, and grieves when you suffer the consequences of your actions.

Sex is more than physical. It is a tri-dimensional experience: spirit, soul, and body. I Corinthians 6:16, 18 (NASB) says, *"Or do you not know that the one who joins himself to a prostitute is one body with her? For He says, "The two shall become one flesh. Flee immorality."*

soul ties

Anytime you have sex with a person you bond with them. You become one and a soul tie is created. A soul tie is a bond that ties you to a relationship and causes you to become attached and connected to that individual. Soul ties are so powerful that when you sleep with a man outside of marriage, your soul becomes bonded with him as well as every person with whom he has had sex. This is why sex should be exclusively reserved for a husband and wife who are committed to each other. Anything outside of that will have profound consequences in your emotions, spiritual life and may even cause physical harm.

If you have had sex outside of marriage, you have a soul tie and it has to be broken before you are married. If it isn't, you will remain bound to those individuals until it is. (Below is a prayer to help you break that soul tie).

Please understand none of what I'm sharing is to incite guilt or shame. The Bible says in Romans 3:23 (NLT), *"For everyone has sinned; we all fall short of God's standards."* I want you to walk in freedom and be that chaste bride adorned for her husband.

When you repent, because of God's infinite love for you, He redeems, forgives, restores and makes you new. And by His grace, He sees you as a virgin again. Decide from today forward, that you will abstain from sex and become be a virgin to your future husband by saving yourself for him alone.

Understand that temptations will continue to come and you will be faced again and again with the choice to engage in sex outside of marriage. However, before you do, ask yourself the following questions:

- Do I want to deal with a soul tie?
- Do I want to honor God with my body?
- Do I believe I know more about sex than God does?
- Do I want to open the door to the enemy in my life through my sin?
- Do I want to open my spirit to every woman this man has ever slept with?
- Do I want to instill the seed of insecurity into my life?
- Do I want to be riddled with shame and guilt?
- Do I want to be separated from God?
- Do I want to grieve the Holy Spirit?

Being abstinent requires creating boundaries that will safeguard your heart. Find a sister/friend who will hold you accountable. Abstaining from premarital sex won't be easy, but it is possible according to Jude 1:24 (NASB), *"Now to Him who is able to keep you from stumbling, and to make you stand in the presence of His glory blameless with great joy!"*

soul tie prayer

Covenant rights or soul ties are formed when you have sexual intercourse outside of marriage. You become "one flesh" with everyone with whom you are sexually involved. The individual has covenant rights over you, and you over them. That bondage has to be destroyed and broken off of your life. If it isn't, you are still tied to them even after marriage.

When you pray this prayer and believe in your heart, you will break free from those covenant rights and soul ties.

Galatians 5:1 (NKJV) says, *"Stand fast therefore in the liberty by which Christ has made us free, and do not be entangled again with a yoke of bondage."*

> Father, in the name of Jesus, I separate myself from every man I have entered into covenant with through sexual intercourse. I destroy their covenant rights over me in the name of Jesus. I destroy my covenant rights over them in the name of Jesus. Forgive me that I have entered into sexual sin and defiled my temple. I receive my freedom from all guilt and condemnation. I walk away from the past and into Your loving and forgiving arms. Restore my virginity before You. I thank You and give You praise and glory that I have been forgiven and I am now free from being one flesh with anyone but my husband at Your perfect time. In the name of Jesus; Amen!

Having said this prayer, believing it in your heart, God has restored your virginity. Amen!

In the Appendix, you will find a Purity Contract. Read it carefully and if this is a vow you choose to make before God, sign it believing that God will help you keep it. You will also find an excellent resource entitled, "How to Avoid Falling into Sexual Temptations" that will help you keep your vow.

Now, don't go back! Get rid of everything (i.e. gifts, momentums, t-shirts, cards, letters, pictures, etc.) that connected you to him.   Delete the text thread, unfollow him on social media and block his phone number. You have to be intentional and determined to stay free.

"A man of God will have godly intentions and is also pursuing a life of abstinence."

Kim McQuitty
@wifeready

kim mcQuitty

session 4
ready work

Describe what you understand to be the consequences of sex outside of marriage?

Why have you decided to walk in purity until marriage?

If you haven't, why not?

What boundaries have you put in place so you won't enter marriage with sexual regrets, emotional baggage or soul ties?

If you have been sexually active, what steps have you taken to stop and be delivered from the soul ties of those past encounters?

What do you plan to do in order to not yield to sexual temptations?

"God placed parameters around premarital sex to protect you, not to deprive you."

Kim McQuitty

@wifeready

"A condom won't protect your soul."

Lestine Bell
@iamlestinebell

kim mcQuitty

notes

notes

kim mcQuitty

notes

notes

session 5
wife material

5

wife material

"An excellent wife who can find? For her worth is far above jewels."
Proverbs 31:10 (NASB)

"Being a wife requires that you have the characteristics and mindset of a wife. Being married is not just a status, it is a condition of the heart. You can't be single-minded and be married. It's not about you!" *Unsave the Date*, Chapter 4, page 60.

are you a wife?

A wedding doesn't make you a wife; it makes you married. Being a wife is the condition of your heart, not just a marital status. The real you is the life inside of you. Everything you do and think is predicated on the condition of your heart. That's why changing your marital status doesn't make you a wife; the condition of your heart does.

Proverbs 4:23 (NASB), says, *"Watch over your heart with all diligence, for from it flows the springs of life."* Out of your heart flows your thoughts, attitude, and deepest part of your being. It's the way you carry yourself, how you live your life, your values, your lifestyle, and your thought life. Have you ever witnessed a woman who is married and still acts as if she's single? A heart transformation from single to married has not occurred.

When your man finds you, you should already be in wife mode; not in the process of becoming one. Being wife-minded requires you to move from a "me to we" mindset long before you walk down the aisle. No, you aren't functioning in the biblical role of a wife, or playing housewife by living together with no marriage covenant. However, you should be wife-minded, not just operating in girlfriend mode.

Mature women and wives carry themselves differently. Also a wife-minded woman won't allow a man to string her along for years with no plan, direction or commitment. If he isn't mature and marriage-minded, move on.

Godly wives aren't born, they are made. When something is made, there is a process and shaping that must take place. For marriage, it begins with the way you think.

Proverbs 23:7 (NKJV) says, *"For as he thinks in his heart, so is he."*
Begin aligning your thoughts to what the Word of God says
about being that excellent wife spoken of in Proverbs 31.

Realize it's no longer all about you! For the rest of your
life, you will have to take into consideration how decisions are
made that benefit and impact your husband and family. Start
getting mentally prepared for the paradigm shift from being
single to being married. It will require a major adjustment, so
get ready for it.

Begin honing your domestic responsibilities by
learning how to cook and care for a home. Work on your
communication skills. Communication is one of the greatest
challenges in relationships and everyone has their own style.
Learn the art of negotiation and compromise. Neither one of
you can always have their way. Marriage is what you negotiate.
You are always on the same team; you will either win together
or lose together.

Finally, there is a tremendous benefit in being mentored
by Titus 2 woman — a godly woman of faith. You need
someone older and wiser with whom you can share your heart.
The wisdom you glean from her will be a game changer in
and of itself. When the time comes for you to be found, your
husband will find you as that virtuous woman whose price is
far above rubies.

biblical roles

Unless you understand the biblical role God is requiring of you, marriage will leave you in a state of frustration. Marriage is a metaphor of the relationship Christ has with the church. We are called to mirror that relationship. Christ submitted Himself to the Father and loved Him unconditionally. The man mirrors Christ by loving unconditionally, and the woman mirrors Christ by submitting to headship.

Your husband is the head. (Ephesians 5:23). God placed the man as head of the wife; not because he's wiser or smarter, but because it's a part of His divine design. If you try to operate in the position of headship, you are competing with God's design and He will not bless His competition.

I'm not saying you no longer have a life of your own; or no "say so" in the marriage. Neither will you *only* become Mrs. So and So. Far from it. In marriage you are partners in life with the joining of purposes, plans, visions, and dreams. However, God is a God of order. He holds your husband responsible for the family, and he will have to give an account for how he led his family.

Back to the role of submission. Submission is not a "dirty" word. I understand it may sound hard and doesn't sit well in the hearts and minds of some women, especially when a man isn't leading well. However, when you love God, and keep His commandments, your heart is that of Colossians 3:23-24 (NKJV), *"And whatever you do, do it heartily, as to the Lord and not to men, knowing that from the Lord you will receive the reward of the inheritance."* You choosing to submit to your husband will be out of your love and reverence for God even when it's difficult for you to do so.

The innate nature of women to try to usurp the role of leadership over the man started with Eve in the Garden of Eden. (Genesis 3:16). It doesn't come naturally for you to be led so you will have to allow the Holy Spirit to temper that behavior in you.

Remember, biblical submission:

Does not violate the personality God has given you as a woman.

Means following leadership; even in areas you would say, "I actually know better how to do this than you."

Operates on pure faith saying, "I believe God sees, hears and knows all and He will intervene on my behalf."

Means to yield to the authority that has been placed in your life by God.

Does not require you to submit to anything abusive or immoral.

You will have to *decide* to implement the principle of biblical submission in your life and choose to submit by faith. It won't always be easy, but it is possible with God's help.

"You are not
a wife when I
marry you, you
are a wife when
I find you."

John Gray
@realjohngray

"A wife
isn't just a
title, it's a
responsibility."

Danielle Ward
@ilvmarriage

session 5
ready work

What has your mother taught you about marriage?

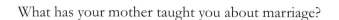

What has your father taught you about men and relationships?

Describe how 'wife ready' you feel you are or are not given the awareness of the responsibility?

List three areas in which you can improve before committing your life to someone else.

What is your greatest fear or concern about being a wife?

What have you done to address this issue?

If you have experienced a divorce, ask God to show you where you may have fallen short when you were a wife?

Make a list of the things you should have done in your marriage.

Make a list of the things you will do differently in your next marriage.

wife material

Being wife material has a set of characteristics and requires a particular mindset. Marriage moves you from "me to we." What do you know about yourself? How can you improve? Take a moment to think about the questions that are posed here. How do you measure up?

> **Are you selfless?** Are you concerned with the needs of others more than yourself? This is vital to the success of your marriage.

> **Are you selfish?** Does everything revolve around you and what you want? Marriage is brutal on selfish people.

> **Are you self-centered?** Do you only think of what's good for you? Marriage is a ministry. Ministry involves serving.

> **Are you responsible?** How well do you take care of your obligations?

> **Are you dependable?** Are you a woman of your word?

> **Can you cook?** You don't have to be a gourmet chef; however, you should know how to put a few meals together.

> **Are you messy?** However tidy you currently are or are not, you will carry those habits into your marriage. It will matter.

100

How are your listening skills? Great communication begins with great listening.

Are you trustworthy? Can you keep your business in your home and between you and your husband?

Are you 'others' conscious? Do you think about others as much as yourself?

How attractive is your personality? Are you sweet and kind; or loud and boisterous?

Do you always have to have the last word? Pride and self-righteousness will keep you vying to have the last word.

"Be the wife
you want to
come home to."

Dr. Laura
@drlauraprogram

kim mcQuitty

notes

notes

kim mcQuitty

notes

are you wife ready? small group curriculum

notes

session 6
marriage

6

marriage

*"Therefore a man shall leave his father and his mother
and hold fast to his wife, and they shall become one flesh."* Genesis 2:24 (NASB)

"Marriage is an institution created by God. *He is the mastermind
behind it and knows how it works best. Why wouldn't you look t*o the
Designer to find out how He intended for it to work? Marriage
is not a do-it-yourself project. Allow the Architect to help you
build something wonderful in your relationship." *Unsave the
Date*, Chapter 5 page 92.

what marriage is not

Marriage is not the end goal or something to check off of your list of lifetime achievements. It's not about life being 'easier' now that you have a partner. It isn't about you having a 'boo thang,' nor no longer being single or finally able to say, "I'm married now." Neither should your marriage be governed by your emotions and opinions.

Marriage isn't for your happiness and what you can get out of the relationship. This couldn't be further from the truth! If you're getting married with your own happiness as your main goal, you will be disappointed severely.

Author Gary Thomas says, "If happiness is our primary goal, we'll get a divorce as soon as happiness seems to wane. But if we marry for the glory of God, to model His love and commitment and to reveal His witness to the world, divorce makes no sense."

Being married is not a guarantee you will never experience loneliness or feeling empty again. That longing and inner craving in your soul is a God-sized hole. Money, sex, food, shopping and even being in a relationship won't fill it. Only God can. He placed it there to keep you coming back to Him. Your husband is not designed to meet all of your needs. He can't! Don't place that kind pressure or unrealistic expectation on another human being. He can't fulfill that for you and you can't fulfill that for him. As I stated earlier, if God isn't enough, no man will ever be.

Frances Moffett, contributor to the Huffington Post shared her thoughts about the realness of marriage on a blog:

"Marriage is not a fairy tale, nor is it an accomplishment or an aspiration. It is not rainbows, fairies, glitter and unicorns. Don't go into marriage with unrealistic expectations, thinking it will save you from your jacked-up life, give you the 'American Dream,' fulfill your emptiness or guarantee stability for you. You don't get married *just* so you can wake up with someone next to you. That ring will not automatically make him change, it will not automatically make you change.

Marriage is real. It's hard work — work that doesn't stop after you've reached a certain milestone. It's a marathon with no finish line (at least until one of you dies). People who are married for decades, don't stay that way by chance. It wasn't that once they hit 10 years, everything was smooth sailing. Sure, it gets easier, but this isn't because time passes. It only gets easier because of the commitment both mates work to make things better."

"Most of us don't *really* talk about marriage until we sit down to *really* talk about marriage.

what marriage is

God created marriage and designed it with a specific purpose and plan. Ignoring His design leads to unnecessary chaos, confusion, pain, and suffering. Unless your marriage is built on truth, it is subject to fail. So many marriages today are built on a broken belief system which is one of the reasons they fail. When a foundation is cracked or broken, whatever is built on it can't help but crumble. Psalm 127:1 (NKJV) says, *"Unless the Lord builds, they labor in vain who build it…"*

Many Christians do not know what a proper marriage should look like, so when they get married, they live out the examples they have seen from their parents, viewed on television, read in a novel or seen in a movie.

Marriage is a covenant, not a contract. The difference between the two is a covenant is permanent and binding; a contract leaves an option for it to be broken.

A covenant is an eternal strategy that says, "I'm in it until death do us part." A contract is an exit strategy that says, "I'm in it until I'm tired of this." In the Kingdom, marriage is like a final sale -- no returns, no exchanges and no refunds. This is God's plan and purpose. Marriage is serious business to God. Once you're married it's for the rest of your life.

When people see your marriage, they should see the love Christ has for His church lived out between you and your husband. The beauty of marriage is a picture of Jesus and His Church (Ephesians 5:21-33). It is a tangible way to show the world what God's love truly looks like. Further, it is an opportunity for God to get the glory out of your life.

112

Jesus sacrificed His life, came to serve, and loves us unconditionally. He is selfless, forgiving and committed to His bride; the Church. Christ made a covenant with us. He still loves us when we're acting all kinds of crazy. He forgives us time after time. He freely lavishes His love on us when we don't deserve it. He didn't come to *be* served but *to* serve. This is what marriage, governed by the Word of God looks like. That is the attitude we should have toward our spouse. The blueprint for your marriage is found in the Word of God. The further away you get from His Word, the harder your marriage will be. You can choose to do marriage your way and get your results, or do it God's way and get His results.

Marriage is about sacrificing, serving, giving and forgiving—and then doing it all over again while enjoying the benefits that come with having a family, companionship, partnership and sexual intimacy.

Adapting God's mindset about marriage will make a huge difference. When your marriage is Christ-centered, everything you do stems from that mindset. You aren't looking to receive, you are seeking to give and to be your husband's helper. This is how to take on the mind of Christ and His heartbeat for your marriage. This is what a marriage after God's own heart will look like!

"Marriage is a ministry and is all about serving. If you don't want to do the work, don't sign up for the gig."

Kim McQuitty
@wifeready

kim mcQuitty

notes

notes

kim mcQuitty

notes

notes

session 6
ready work

Why do you want to get married?

How has your parent's marriage or relationship(s) impacted you?

Why do you believe so much is required of you when you are married, and are you willing to give it?

What does marriage mean to you?

What weaknesses do you bring into your marriage?

What strengths do you bring into your marriage?

Other than attending these small group sessions, what are you doing to prepare yourself for marriage or remarriage?

If you are divorced, what is your greatest concern or fear about being remarried?

What have you done to address this?

"Marriage is like a marathon with no finish line. You don't quit because it hurts, you have to push through and keep going. You signed up until death do you part, not until I'm tired of this."

Kim McQuitty
@wifeready

kim mcQuitty

notes

are you wife ready? small group curriculum

notes

kim mcQuitty

notes

notes

session 7
final thoughts

7

final thoughts

"For this reason a man shall leave his father and his mother, and be joined to his wife; and they shall become one flesh." Genesis 2:24 (NASB)

"The marriage relationship is wonderful, romantic, exciting, rewarding and life-giving. I highly recommend all women to experience it. There is nothing on earth like being in love with the love of your life." - *Unsave the Date*, Afterword, Page 97.

I pray this *Wife Ready* curriculum has enriched your life and shed some insight on being a wife after God's own heart. This information is something I wish I had before I said, "I do," as did many of my friends who have shared their hearts on the matter. Had I personally known then, what I know now, I may not have gotten married so young." Armed with this knowledge, I would have done the necessary work on myself first to become a better *me* before becoming *we*.

Remember, being a "wife" begins long before you are married, and it begins with you. The steps you have taken over the past seven weeks to work on yourself is one of the best decisions you could have made. As the late Maya Angelo said, "When you know better, you do better." Your commitment to this journey has positioned you to enter marriage with your eyes wide open.

Working on yourselves is something you and your husband will have to do throughout your marriage. According to Paul David Tripp, "One of the best ways to improve your marriage is to draw a circle around yourself and work on changing everyone inside the circle." If you adopt this mindset and perspective early on, the better your marriage will be.

Allow the Holy Spirit to show you where you need to work on yourself when challenges or hardships arise in your relationship. You can't change anyone in the relationship except you. The focus should always be on working on yourself, not trying to fix your husband.

Marriage is a wonderful, deeply satisfying and fulfilling relationship with a love like no other. I want you to win at it! I want your marriage to be your best "Yes." You deserve to have that deep love and intimacy that is shared between a husband and wife. Marriage is meant to be enjoyed not endured.

You are ready now more than you've ever been. Continue to prepare by reading books, growing and working on yourself. Don't stop now; so when you get married, your husband will have a whole, healed, happy and complete woman of God who is the highest expression of herself.

You won't be looking for him to make you happy, rather he will share in your existing happiness and create more of it with you.

This is the state of being *wife ready*!

kim mcQuitty

dear wife-to-be...

Wait. Wait for him...

Wait for the one who cherishes you. The man who brings out the best in you. The one who will stop at nothing to be with you, no matter the circumstances. The man who makes you smile like no other has or can.

Wait for the man who will love you just as you are. The one who will make you a priority. The one who loves having you by his side. And most of all, wait for the one who will love you as Christ loves the church.

Before that long-awaited day comes, make up in your mind you are going to do marriage God's way. In these lessons, you learned that marriage is far more than having a man and a wedding. It is a covenant vow you will make before God. Know it will take a considerable amount of work and intentionality if you want it to thrive.

During the lifetime of your marriage, there will be times when you won't feel like you want to be married. You won't want to be supportive. You won't feel as if your husband deserves to be respected. This is why love isn't reason enough to get married.

Love is a decision, not a feeling. Love is a commitment and a covenant made with God. Just like He made a covenant with you and still loves, forgives and is committed to you when you don't deserve it, you are required to do the same.

There are so many wonderful, fun and memorable moments ahead. Enjoy them. Take them in. Choose to live in the moment. Just as you have great times ahead, trials and temptations will arise, as well. Remember why you chose him. Remember why you waited for him. Remember why you married him. Remember why you said no to the other 3.5 billion men on the planet and yes to him. Remember you took a vow; you made a covenant.

Understand when things aren't right in your relationship with your husband, something is out of alignment in your relationship with God. You are the only person you can change in your marriage. Always work on yourself instead of pointing fingers at your husband.

Live legacy minded. Have the marriage your kids will aspire to have. You can't hurry up and have a legacy. Legacies take time to build. You are building one; good or bad. Aim to build a great one.

You made a wonderful decision to invest in your marriage by spending the last seven weeks gaining an understanding of that to which you are committing your lifetime. As you continue your journey, stay in the Word of God. That's where your wisdom and direction will come from.

In closing, thank you for spending this time with me. Thank you for trusting me with your heart. Thank you for allowing me to serve you in the capacity in which God has mandated me to do, which is to help his daughters get ready for marriage.

I pray you now see and better understand marriage from God's perspective. I pray you esteem your worth and value, and know not just any man can have you; only the one who *gets* to marry you!

Much love,

Kim McQuitty

Author/Speaker

Follow @wifeready on Instagram and Facebook. Check out my blog at www.areyouwifeready.com. Email me at info@wifeready.org to share how this curriculum has impacted you. I'd love to hear from you!

are you wife ready? small group curriculum

notes

kim mcQuitty

notes

notes

kim mcQuitty

notes

are you wife ready? small group curriculum

notes

appendix

affirmations

Your words have power that changes circumstances and shapes destinies! Speak these affirmations over your life daily and watch yourself transform. What you repeatedly hear, you will eventually believe.

I am somebody!

I am who God says I am!

Though every man might lie, God's Word is always true!

I am on top and never beneath!

I am the head and not the tail!

I am the lender and not the borrower!

I am blessed in the city and blessed in the field!

I am blessed in my coming and blessed in my going!

I am not an accident!

I have a purpose and a destiny to fulfill!

I do not receive words that are not of God which have been spoken over my life!

I send all words of death and destruction back to hell where they came from!

I daily confess God's Word over my life!

I am an heir of God and a joint heir with Christ Jesus!

I have been fearfully and wonderfully created by God!

I have great worth and great value!

My worth is far above rubies and pearls!

I am a child of God!

I love God and am loved by God!

I have a peace that passes all of man's understanding!

I am a royal priesthood; I am a peculiar person!

I am favored of the Lord!

I am beautiful inside and out!

I have an anointing on my life that is growing every day!

I am bold as a lion!

I am healthy, wealthy and wise!

kim mcQuitty

how to avoid falling
into sexual temptation

maintain a daily devotion in God's Word

God primarily speaks to us through His Word. Develop a daily habit of spending time in Scripture so you can discern the voice of God. You will be empowered to resist situations that are not beneficial for you.

> Hebrews 4:12 (NASB): *"For the word of God is living and active and sharper than any two-edged sword, and piercing as far as the division of soul and spirit, of both joints and marrow, and able to judge the thoughts and intentions of the heart."*

be wise when using social media

Social media is a tool. Using it to connect with old boyfriends can open the door to trouble. Be wise and keep the door closed. Don't entertain the inbox message or respond to any posts on your feed.

> 2 Timothy 2:22 (NASB): *"Now flee from youthful lusts and pursue righteousness, faith, love and peace with those who call on the Lord from a pure heart."*

don't put yourself in tempting situations

Stay away from certain people or places that may stir up ungodly longings.

> 1 Corinthians 6:18-20 (NLT): *"Run from sexual sin! No other sin so clearly affects the body as this one does. For sexual immorality is a sin against your own body. Don't you realize your body is the temple of the Holy Spirit who lives in you and was given to you by God? You do not belong to yourself, for God bought you with a high price. So you must honor God with your body."*

kim mcQuitty

get an accountability partner

Accountability partners can help keep you from stumbling.
Entrust yourself to a friend who will hold you accountable
and ask you the tough questions.

Proverbs 27:17 (NASB): *"Iron sharpens iron, So one man sharpens another…"*

ask for prayer if you feel tempted

Reach out and ask for prayer to help you from succumbing to
temptation. There is power in agreement.

Luke 22:40b (NASB): *"…pray that you may not enter into temptation."*

develop a consistent prayer life

Spend time daily talking to God. Your time in prayer will
establish a sensitivity to the Holy Spirit's conviction that will
empower you to resist temptation when it arises.

Ephesians 6:18 (NKJV): *"Praying always with all prayer and supplication in the Spirit, being watchful to this end with all perseverance and supplication for all the saints."*

create boundaries with the opposite sex

Avoid sharing intimate details of your life that would form a heart connection with a male friend. Once a bond is formed, it will be hard to break, and even harder if he becomes involved with someone else. Save yourself this heartache.

Proverbs 4:23 (NKJV): *"Keep your heart with all diligence, for out of it spring the issues of life."*

remind yourself of the consequences

Consider the results if you gave into your temptation, and the consequences brought on your life and your relationship with God.

James 1:13-15 (NASB): *"And remember, when you are being tempted, do not say, "God is tempting me." God is never tempted to do wrong, and he never tempts anyone else. Temptation comes from our own desires, which entice us and drag us away. These desires give birth to sinful actions. And when sin is allowed to grow, it gives birth to death."*

when the temptation occurs, immediately remove yourself.

Whether it may be on social media, or an office relationship, or a shared ministry at church - remove yourself from the tempting situation and choose not to feed it.

> 2 Timothy 2:22 (NLT): *"Run from anything that stimulates youthful lusts. Instead, pursue righteous living, faithfulness, love, and peace. Enjoy the companionship of those who call on the Lord with pure hearts."*

keep yourself occupied

Proverbs 16:27 (TLB): *"Idle hands are the devil's workshop; idle lips are his mouthpiece."* Comedian George Carlin added, "An idle mind is the devil's workshop." A lack of useful things to do is the breeding ground of much wrong doing. Keep yourself engaged in wholesome activities. This will decrease idle time to contemplate situations or the urge to follow through on them.

> I Thessalonians 5:11(NLT): *"So encourage each other and build each other up, just as you are already doing."*

purity contract

I _____

on this day _____

vow to remain abstinent until I am married. I understand that sex is a gift between a man and woman and is ordained by God for the covenant of marriage. I trust that in God's timing He will bring the husband He has for me. I will not put myself in compromising situations where I will be tempted. I will take impure thoughts to God. I know I can remain pure with God's help because He will strengthen me. (Philippians 4:13)

Signature _____

questions to ask before you say, "I do"

It is very important for couples who plan to get married to know if they are actually compatible. Below are questions you should ask one another before marriage so you'll know where each other stands.

love/sex/romance

What would be left of our relationship if we eliminated physical attraction?

What is the best way I can show you that I love you?

What is it I do that causes you to question my love for you?

If we couldn't have children for medical reasons, how would our relationship be affected?

What are your thoughts on only having sex with me for the rest of your life?

What is your love language?

How will we continue to date after we are married?

the past

What experiences from your childhood influence your behavior and attitude? In what way?

What could cause feelings of affection and romance to be revived if you met a previous boyfriend/girlfriend, even though you feel strongly committed to me?

What are things from your past you are afraid to share with me?

What didn't you like about any previous partners?

What letters or memorabilia have you kept from past relationships? Why have you kept them?

How would you feel if there are things in my past I'm not willing to share with you?

154

Was there any abuse; emotionally, sexually, verbally or physically, by your mother or father towards you in any way?

Was either of your parents abusive to the other?

Have you ever been sexually abused? If so, to whom did you report it?

What bad habits have you had to overcome? How long did you deal with them and when were you freed from them?

Have you ever been involved in any criminal activities? What were they?

What role did violence play in any past relationships?

Have you ever been in jail or prison? If so, why and for how long were you sentenced?

Are you presently maintaining relationships with your past boyfriend/girlfriends? If so, would you end it for me if I felt uncomfortable?

What was the reason your past relationship ended?

trust

What are your thoughts on trust?

What behaviors have I exhibited that made you feel uncomfortable with my behavior with the opposite sex?

What have I done or could do to cause you to not trust me?

Which should come first; your spouse or the children?

How do you feel about my trustworthiness with handling money?

How do you feel about us opening each other's mail?

Tell me about a time when your trust was broken in a past relationship. What were the events that caused your trust for someone to be broken? What happened between us that caused your trust of me to be broken?

Have you ever been cheated on?

Have you ever cheated on anyone? If so, why?

the future

What do you see as our major differences?

How do our differences complement us?

How can our differences become a source of future conflict?

What does spending time with your friends, family and work colleagues look like for you?

How did your family resolve conflicts in your home growing up? Do you disapprove or approve of it was handled? Why?

What changes, if any will you make to resolve conflicts in our future family?

kim mcQuitty

What frightens you about marriage?

Where would you prefer to live; in the suburbs, city, or country? Why?

How would you feel if I was offered a big promotion at work that would require us to relocate away from our families?

What are your thoughts if I travel on my own to visit family, pursue a hobby, or deal with stress?

What are your feelings on marriage counseling if we are experiencing trouble in our marriage?

If the need arises, how do you feel about our parents having to live with us?

What do you feel like you will be sacrificing the most to marry me?

If you marry me, what would you regret not accomplishing or being able to do?

How will we spend the holidays?

children

How many children do you want?

How do you feel about adoption if we can't conceive or as a means to adding additional children to our family?

How long would you like to wait before having children?

When we have children, how will we divide the responsibility in caring for them?

What types of discipline do you encourage to correct their behavior?

How do you feel about taking in a relative's child to raise, if we had to?

If we determine the child(ren) won't go to daycare, how will we determine who will stay home?

annoyances

What don't you like about me?

What constitutes nagging for you?

How does nagging make you feel? When do you feel I nag?

How do you feel about the way I dress? What would you like to see change?

How do I annoy you?

Who in my family annoys you?

What does my family do that annoys you?

What if anything, do you do, in your line of work that I would disapprove of or could potentially hurt me?

How do you feel about staying a marriage even if you are unhappy all the time?

When do you need personal space away from me?

communication

How should we handle any difficult feelings about each other?

If you always say you are going to do something, but never do it, what is the best way to bring this problem to your attention?

What did you admire about the way your mother and father treated each other?

What is the best way for me to communicate difficult feelings about you, to you, and not cause an offense?

What makes you not want to talk to me?

Do you feel you can talk with me about any subject?

What do you fear about communicating your feelings?

What causes you to shut down?

finances

What justifies us going into debt?

How much debt do you have?

How do you feel when financial problems arise?

How do you use your credit cards?

What's the best way to prepare for financial emergencies?

Is a lack of money a good enough reason to not have children?

When our child(ren) is/are born, how do you feel about them going to daycare?

Are you a spender or a saver?

Do you have budget?

What percentage of your check should be saved?

Which one of us will handle the bills?

How much debt do you have?

How do you feel about my debt becoming our debt?

Will we have joint or separate bank accounts? Why?

How much money do you have in the bank?

Are you comfortable with transferring your money in a joint account after marriage?

What is your credit score?

What are your thoughts about helping family or friends financially?

Are you in debt to the IRS?

miscellaneous

To whom are you closest, your mother or father? Why?

What do you fear?

What are your thoughts on our parents knowing if we aren't doing well financially?

What are your views and thoughts about pornography?

How would you react if our son or daughter told us they are gay?

What are your feelings on racial prejudice?

Will we have guns in our home?

What health problems do you have?

What medications do you currently take?

What psychological or mental health challenges have you experienced?

Has anyone in your family had any mental health challenges? If so, who and what?

Have you ever been addicted to drugs, alcohol, or any other substance? How did you overcome your addiction?

Have you been in rehab for treatment for any type of addiction?

How do you operate when you are in a bad mood? How should I deal with it?

How do you feel about us having a pet? If you want a pet, what type?

What church will we attend?

How would your feelings change towards me if I gained weight?

What kind of marriage will we have?

What are your thoughts on us investing in our relationship by attending marriage conferences and retreats?

31 prayers for my future husband

The greatest thing a wife can do is pray for her husband, and before you say, "I do" is the time to begin! It is a privilege and responsibility to cover him daily in prayer. This is a vital spiritual discipline and must be exercised throughout the course of your marriage.

Praying God's will and Word is powerful! Astounding manifestations will happen in your husband's life when you pray for him. There is power in sowing the seed of the Word of God because He watches over His Word to perform it. (Jeremiah 1:12)

spiritual life

Matthew 6:33 (NASB): *"But seek first His kingdom and His righteousness and all these things will be added to you."*

Father, I pray my husband will be a disciple of Jesus Christ. I pray the spiritual disciplines of prayer, fasting, and studying the Word will be his lifestyle. May he always seek You first.

wisdom

James 1:5 (NASB): *"But if any of you lacks wisdom, let him ask of God, who gives to all generously and without reproach and it will be given to him."*

Father, I pray my husband is a man of wisdom. When he lacks direction, may he always inquire of You and not lean on his own understanding.

humility

Psalm 51:10 (NASB): *"Create in me a clean heart, O God, and renew a steadfast spirit with me."*

Lord, I pray my husband will be humble and quick to agree with You about his sin. May his heart always will be tender toward Your voice.

leadership

Ephesians 5:23 (NASB): *"For the husband is the head of the wife, as Christ also is the head of the church, He Himself being the Savior of the body."*

Father, I pray my husband will continually grow in his leadership abilities as he leads our family so You will be glorified.

inordinate affections

Romans 13:14 (NIV): *"Let us behave decently, as in the daytime, not in carousing and drunkenness, not in sexual immorality and debauchery, not in dissension and jealousy."*

Father, I pray you will safeguard my husband's heart against inappropriate relationships. Thank you that his heart will be pure and undivided in his commitment to You and our family.

character

Proverbs 22:1 (NASB): *"A good name is to be more desired than great wealth, favor is better than silver and gold."*

Father, I pray my husband's character will precede him. Through his good character, help him establish a respected and honorable name by being a man of his word. May You get the glory out of his life in all he endeavors to do.

finances

Proverbs 21:20 (AMP): *"There is precious treasure and oil in the house of the wise [who prepare for the future], But a short-sighted and foolish man swallows it up and wastes it."*

Lord, I thank you for giving my husband wisdom in the area of finances. I ask you to help him handle all aspects of finances wisely. May he be a good steward over what you have entrusted to him. I pray our finances will not be a source of contention in our marriage. May he have a heart to further advance the Kingdom with the resources you have blessed him with.

integrity

Proverbs 10:9 (NASB): *"He who walks in integrity walks securely, but he who perverts his ways will be found out."*

Father, I pray my husband will cultivate strong integrity, and not compromise his convictions. I pray he will be honest in his business dealings, and will never do anything he needs to hide from me, or from others.

teachable spirit

I Peter 5:5 (NASB): *"…clothe yourselves with humility toward one another, for God is opposed to the proud, but gives grace to the humble."*

Father, I pray that my husband will always have a teachable spirit. When he is uncertain about various situations may he not walk in pride, but admit his limitations and inability to others who can teach and help him.

sexuality

Song of Solomon 7:10 (NASB): *"I am my beloved's and his desire is for me."*

Father, I pray my husband recognizes the sexual drive You placed in him is to keep him coming back to me. I pray he will exercise self-control and never yield to any temptations. I pray our sexual intimacy, when we are married, will be a reflection of selfless love.

friends

Proverbs 13:20 (NASB): *"He who walks with wise men will be wise, But the companion of fools will suffer harm."*

Lord, Your Word tells us bad company corrupts good character. I pray my husband will choose God-honoring friendships - individuals who will add value to his life and not lead him into sin.

accountability

Proverbs 27:17 (NASB): *"Iron sharpens iron, so one man sharpens another."*

Father, I ask that you give my husband a heart to have godly men to whom he makes himself accountable. Send men who will speak truth into his life, strong men of faith who will cover him in prayer.

anger

Ephesians 4:26 (NASB): *"Be angry, and yet do not sin; do not let the sun go down on your anger."*

Lord, I pray my husband will be patient and a man of peace. I pray he will manage his anger without sin, and allow the Holy Spirit to help control his responses.

temptation

2 Corinthians 10:5 (NKJV): *"...casting down arguments and every high thing that exalts itself against the knowledge of God, bringing every thought into captivity to the obedience of Christ."*

Father, I pray my husband will yield his mind and thoughts to You. I pray he will take every immoral and impure thought captive and resist the temptation to indulge in pornography and other lustful activities.

forgiveness

Ephesians 4:32 (NASB): *"Be kind to one another, tenderhearted, forgiving each other, just as God in Christ has also forgiven you."*

Lord, I pray my husband will choose to walk in forgiveness. Give him a revelation that any bitterness, resentment or unforgiving attitude will block the flow of blessings in his life. May he always be tender-hearted and forgiving remembering that you forgave him.

fatherhood

Colossians 3:21 (AMP): "*Fathers, do not provoke or irritate or exasperate your children [with demands that are trivial or unreasonable or humiliating or abusive; nor by favoritism or indifference; treat them tenderly with lovingkindness], so they will not lose heart and become discouraged or unmotivated [with their spirits broken].*"

Lord I pray my husband will be a good father to our children. Even if he hasn't had an earthly example of what a father is, I pray he submits himself to being fathered by You. May he not provoke our children to anger. May he discipline them wisely and love them unconditionally.

fear of God

Proverbs: 15:33 (NASB): "*The fear of the Lord is the instruction for wisdom, And before honor comes humility.*"

God, I pray my husband will have a reverential fear of You. May his heart always aim to please you and obey what You have commanded in Scripture.

identity in Christ

Colossians 2:10 (NASB): *"...and in Him you have been made complete."*

The Bible says if any man be in Christ, he is a new creation. I pray my husband will know he is complete in You and aligns himself with what the Word says about him.

authority as a believer

Luke 10:19 (NASB): *"Behold, I have given you authority to tread on serpents and scorpions, and over all the power of the enemy, and nothing will injure you."*

Lord, when the enemy comes to wage war against our marriage, I pray my husband will know the authority he walks in and exercise the power you have given him over the power of the enemy.

purpose

Jeremiah 29:11 (NASB): *"For I know the plans that I have for you, declares the Lord, plans for welfare and not for calamity to give you a future and a hope."*

Lord, thank you for the plans you have for my husband, I pray my husband will walk in his God-given purpose, reach his full potential, and pursue only those goals that will bring You glory.

health

1 Corinthians 6:19-20 (NASB): *"Or do you not know that your body is a temple of the Holy Spirit who is in you, whom you have from God and that you are not your own? For you have been bought with a price; therefore, glorify God in your body."*

God, I pray my husband will understand the importance of taking care of his body—the temple of the Holy Spirit—for Your glory. I pray he will practice self-control by making wise food choices, and get sufficient exercise to stay healthy, and sufficient rest to be strong in life and in You.

prayer life

I Thessalonians 5:17 (NASB): *"...pray without ceasing."*

I pray my husband will be a man of prayer. As the spiritual leader of our home, let him lead us according to Your plan for our lives. I pray he will possess a lifestyle of prayer and communion with You.

fears

2 Timothy 1:7 (NKJV): *"For God has not given us a spirit of fear, but of power and of love and of a sound mind."*

Lord, you have repeatedly said in your Word to "fear not." I cover my husband in prayer that those fears he may fight will not overtake him. I declare that no weapon of fear that is formed against him will prosper in his life. Give him a revelation of the perfect love You have for him.

choices

Proverbs 19:21(NKJV): *"Many are the plans in the mind of a man, but it is the purpose of the Lord that will stand."*

Lord, you have given each one of us a free will. I pray my husband's choices will always be in alignment with Your Word. May he be sensitive to Your voice and choose to obey Your commandments.

protection

Psalm 91:1 (NKJV): *"He who dwells in the shelter of the Most High will abide in the shadow of the Almighty."*

Father, I draw a bloodline - the shed blood of Jesus - around my husband. I pray for divine protection over him. Let your ministering angels be encamped around him. Let him dwell in the secret place of the Most High and abide under the shadow of the Almighty.

past

Philippians 3:13-14 (NKJV): *"...forgetting what lies behind, and reaching forward to what lies ahead. I press on toward the goal for the prize of the upward call of God in Christ Jesus."*

Father, I pray my husband receives the forgiveness you have given to him and that he will not allow his past to impact what you have for him in the future.

relationship with his father

Mark 11:25 (NIV): *"And when you stand praying, if you hold anything against anyone, forgive them, so that your Father in heaven may forgive you your sins."*

Father, I pray if there is any contention in the relationship with my husband and his father, that you will bring healing. Let there be forgiveness, reconciliation, and restoration. If the relationship with his father is healthy, let them continue to build that life-giving relationship between a father and his son.

fatherless son

Psalm 68:5 (NKJV): *"A father to the fatherless…"*

Lord, I pray if my husband has never had a relationship with his father or doesn't know who he is, that You will bring healing to that hole in his heart. Let him become aware his identity is in You. Heal that ache in his heart that longs for his earthly father so he can be fathered by You.

priorities

Matthew 6:33 (NKJV): *"But seek first His kingdom and His righteousness, and all these things will be added to you."*

God, I pray my husband will understand family priorities. May he always put You first, his family second and work/ministry third.

mind

Isaiah 26:3 (NKJV): *"You will keep him in perfect peace whose mind is stayed on you because he trusts in you."*

I pray my husband has a sound mind. I pray he casts out every thought that does not line up with your Word. May he keep his mind on you, as you keep him in Your perfect peace.

favor

Luke 2:52 (NASB): *"And Jesus kept increasing in wisdom and stature, and in favor with God and man."*

Father, I pray your favor would surround my husband like a shield. I decree and declare that he is increasing in wisdom, favor and stature with God and with men.

about the author

Kim McQuitty is an author, speaker, mentor and premarital coach, who has been encouraging women through ministry for over 25 years. She challenges and inspires them to maximize their potential and walk in their God-appointed purpose by fulfilling Christ's mandate for their lives. Many have been touched by her pragmatic, influential messages that transform lives, heal hearts, and win souls for Jesus Christ. Her vision is for ordinary women to become extraordinary women of distinction, worth, emotional wholeness and Kingdom excellence.

Through her commitment in helping women and her passion for marriage, Kim founded *Wife Ready* to help women prepare for marriage beyond the wedding day. Her mission is to equip and empower women, impart wisdom, and practical habits to them so they can become better prepared for the marathon of marriage. Kim resides in Atlanta and has 2 adult daughters.

end notes

1. William Shakespeare https://www.brainyquote.com/quotes/william_shakespeare_106104

2. Les Parrott, Ph.D. states in his book, *Saving Your Marriage Before it Starts*, "Marriage won't make you happy, you make marriage happy."

3. How Many Men Are in the World? https://www.reference.com/world-view/many-men-world-8e066f56a72027ce

4. Focus on the Family, God's Design for Marriage https://www.focusonthefamily.com/marriage/gods-design-for-marriage/

5. We Need to More Honest About the Realness of Marriage https://www.huffpost.com/entry/we-need-to-be-more-honest-about-the-realness-of-marriage_b_58ea9739e4b00dd8e016ed3b

6. Mayo Angelo, https://quotefancy.com/quote/759763/Maya-Angelou-When-you-know-better-you-do-better

7. Paul David Tripp, https://www.azquotes.com/author/21823-Paul_David_Tripp

8. Comedian George Carlin, https://www.brainyquote.com/authors/george-carlin-quotes

Made in the USA
Columbia, SC
26 June 2020